KU-268-613

*Daro Montag* THIS EARTH

LEEDS COLLEGE OF ART AND DESIGN

LRC
BLENHEIM WALK
LEEDS LS2 9AQ
T

*Daro Montag*  THIS EARTH

LEEDS COL OF ART & DESIGN

R50620L0084

Published by Festerman Press 2007

In association with the RANE Research Cluster, University College Falmouth

ISBN 978-0-9544187-4-8

All images and text © Daro Montag

All rights reserved. This book, or any part thereof, may not be reproduced,
in any form or by any means, without the prior permission of the author.

Designed by Robin Hawes

Printed by R. Booth Ltd.
Mabe, Cornwall

R50620
LEEDS COLLEGE OF ART & DESIGN
28.2.08
LRC
735.29
DAW

Soil has played an important role in numerous works of art. Since humans first daubed their handprints on cave walls – the earliest surviving paintings – the colour of earth has been an essential medium. Different coloured soils, and their mineral constituents, originally provided the pigment for a large range of paints and, once it was discovered that clay could be modelled and hardened, it also became used for representational and well as utilitarian purposes.

In more recent times, soil once again became a key medium for sculptors. In the 1970s, a number of prominent artists created works away from the confines of the gallery. Instead of producing sculpture for urban environments, artists such as Walter de Maria, Michael Heizer and Robert Morris used vast tracts of remote land as the site for new works. Using diggers and bulldozers, these 'land artists', as they became known, gouged out tons of mud and rock to create massive earthworks.

Although this work was being created at a time of growing environmental awareness, this was not their core concern. Issues of art and its placement were often their overriding motivation; earth was being used for its sculptural qualities, rather than as a living substance.

By focusing on its formal materiality, such works tend to ignore or deny the life-sustaining qualities of soil. In 1977, for example, Walter de Maria filled a New York gallery with 250 cubic yards of earth. The sculpture, known as *New York Earth Room*, covers 3,600 square feet of floor space to a depth of 22 inches. Its indoor presence is somewhat disconcerting and, as an installation, it confronts the viewer with both its emptiness and its potential.

This amount of soil contains unimaginable numbers of organisms. It is rich in colour and life. Even a small sample is packed with micro-organisms – seeds, fungal spores, nematodes and other microbes. They lie dormant, waiting for some moisture that will enable them to spring into life. Consequently, the gallery needs to maintain this installation in a state of suspended animation, and any weeds that begin to sprout are swiftly removed. So *Earth Room* is more about sculpture than ecology.

Visiting this installation for the first time, in 1996, I couldn't help imagining how different it would look if the fire sprinklers were accidentally triggered. The water would enliven the soil's potential, forgotten seeds would germinate from the brown and barren field, and instead of an expanse of

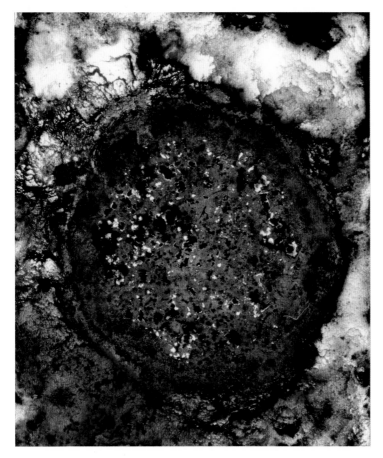

Daro Montag *Earth Room Earth*,
1996. 5.4 film, soil from Walter de
Maria's *New York Earthroom*,
microbes.

mud, we might see drifts of grasses or wild flowers, or maybe some seedling trees breaking through the crust.

The soil, however, has not been watered. Confronted by this absence of visible life, I took a small sample, with the permission of the gallery, and used it to create a Bioglyph.[1] Within days of it being placed on the surface of some moist film, plants and fungi began to emerge and smaller organisms were beginning to stir. Within two weeks, this micro-community had thrived and left its trace in the coloured gelatin. The resulting print, made from this decomposed piece of film, was later exhibited a few doors down from the Dia Art Foundation that houses *New York Earth Room*[2].

This approach, which views soil as a *prima materia*[3] as opposed to a mere sculptural material, is related more to 'ecological' art than 'land' or 'environmental' practices.[4] In contrast to the land art of the 1970s, a number of artists working concurrently produced art that drew attention to the symbolic and essential life-sustaining properties of soil.

These forerunners were to inspire much subsequent ecological art. They include Alan Sonfist, herman de vries, Ana Mendieta and Paolo Barrile. Barrile, in particular, has made it his mission to raise our awareness of soil through his *Message Earth* project. Since 1969, he has been salvaging uncontaminated earth as well as initiating pressure-group activity and other consciousness-raising initiatives.[5]

Since this initial adoption of ecological ideas, there is now a new generation of artists who examine the biological, chemical and even alchemical properties of soil. Many collaborate with scientists or specialists from other disciplines. The overarching idea that links many of these diverse projects has been the desire to raise public awareness of the importance of healthy soil, to draw attention to its significance and to celebrate its vitality. This small publication records one such project.

1  The term 'Bioglyph' refers to the method of making images first devised by Daro Montag in 1993. Essentially it is process by which micro-organisms are encouraged to leave a trace of their activities on colour film. They are not photographs, but direct records of micro-biological activity. For further information and a theoretical exposition of this practice see: *Bioglyphs: The generation of images in collaboration with nature's events*, Daro Montag, PhD thesis, University of Hertfordshire, 2000.

2  This work, entitled *Earth Room Earth*, was first exhibited at Caren Golden Fine Art, NY, in 1997.

3  *Prima Materia* is the primitive formless base of all matter. In the broadest terms the concept of the prima materia states that all particular substances are formed out of one and the same original substance.

4  The contrast between Bioglyphs and Land Art was first noted in *Nature tracing itself: Chris Townsend on Daro Montag's Bioglyphs* – Hotshoe, May-June 2000.

5  For further information about artists working in various ways with soil see: *www.kunstundboden.de*.

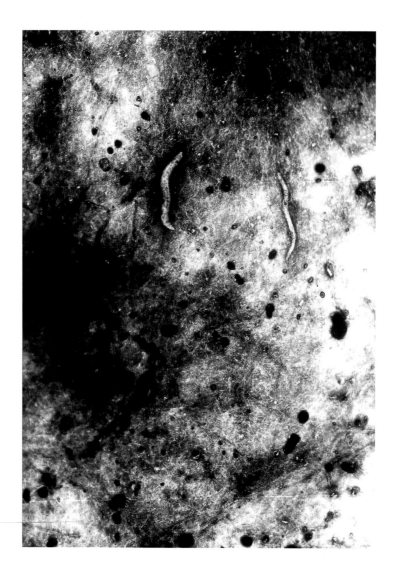

*'It remains the sobering fact that even in the age of global communications and the Internet, civilisation continues to depend on a few inches of topsoil for its very existence. The activity in and around that soil provides the material to sustain life and the environment to give it meaning. The earth is very forgiving of our abuse. But it will not forgive forever.'*

Graham Harvey, *The Killing of the Countryside*

## KNOWING MY PLACE

The term 'oekologie' (ecology) was initially coined in 1866 by the German biologist Ernst Haeckel. Since its derivation comes from the two Greek words meaning 'household' and 'study', the term literally means 'the study of the household'. Although the word is now used more widely to suggest a form of environmental knowledge that is generally holistic and systemic, I would like to dwell for a short while on its original sense – of studying the home.

In the current rush towards globalisation, our attention is often diverted from our surrounding location. With recent developments in mass media and global communication, it is easy to have a superficial knowledge of events on the other side of the planet, and yet have no knowledge of one's own, immediate environment. This superficiality is symptomatic of our modern malaise that has cast us adrift from a healthy relationship with nature.

It seems important, therefore, for an ecological artist to develop a deeper knowledge of his or her own habitat, and to use that knowledge to feed their practice. This is not to rule out work about other ecological niches, but to suggest that, before rushing off to fix other people's environments, it might be good to have gained a thorough working knowledge of one's own place on this planet. Consequently, I believe it is important for anyone interested in ecology to spend some time concentrating on, and learning about, their own immediate locality.

This notion of 'knowing your place' applies regardless of where you happen to live. It is just as relevant to an urban setting as to a rural one.

Our environment is everywhere – indeed, it is wherever we are. Over the past few years, my own particular habitat has become central to my art practice. It is more than just a source of inspiration; it is a co-creator, a generator of artworks.

Rather than create art that simply portrays this particular location in south-west Cornwall, known as Lower Treculliacks, I have chosen to work more in collaboration with the place. In doing so, I have come to under-stand that place is not a singular entity. It is complex, many layered and, for the most part, hidden from our perception. Instead of referring to the concept of a fixed location, 'place' seems to be more of a nexus where events unfold. It is made up of plants, animals, people, buildings, weather systems, stories, dreams – and all their never-ending interactions. It is always chang-ing, regardless of anything we may do. In trying to understand a place in this way, I have become more enmeshed in its multi-dimensionality.

In order to engage more fully with the innumerable features that make up Lower Treculliacks, I chose to start at the bottom, with the soil. As Graham Harvey reminds us, although the soil can seem a lowly or insignif-icant medium to our 21st-century technology, without a few inches of good topsoil our civilisation would crumble. The soil, then, would seem like a good starting point for getting to know one's place on this planet.

## Looking at mud

We often speak about soil as though it were just one thing, a separate entity in the world. But, as any gardener will tell you, this is far from the truth. Nothing is fixed, and the humble earth is no exception. Soil is many things and there are many different soils. In one of the earliest books on soil, entitled *Terra* (1675), John Evelyn states that the theorists of his day "reckon up no fewer than one hundred seventy nine millions one thousand and sixty different sorts of Earths".[6]

While the precise number of different soils may not be possible to calculate, there are certain key components that all soils have in common. How we choose to think about these components is likely to say as much about our personal interests as the soil itself. Each discipline will highlight some aspects and ignore others. The biologist, for example, will be interested in the organic matter that is contained within the soil. The geologist, on the other hand, might be more interested in its mineral components, and be able to unravel from these the history of its formation. The horticulturist will analyse the soil as a medium that supports plants. The poet will draw attention to its symbolic connotations, while the painter might take inspiration from its rich palette of colours.

Although little more than one acre, much of the soil at Lower Treculliacks has been untouched for decades. While the garden that surrounds the house has been well tended, the small field, known as *Stony Acre*, was uncultivated and overgrown. The topsoil is, in many places, around 40 centimetres deep and slightly acidic. Its colour, according to the Munsell system, is composed of a range of browns, including 'brown', 'dark greyish brown' or 'very dark greyish brown'.[7] This would indicate that the soil is generally rich in organic matter and has a high carbon content.

The organic content is clearly visible to the naked eye. Small fragments of decaying plant matter – roots, bark, leaves – have been pulled well below the surface by the activities of earthworms. In samples of the topsoil viewed under a scanning electron microscope, the difference between the organic and the inorganic, between plant and mineral, is even more apparent.

Although most of the individual organic particles are tiny, when added together they are massive. The implications of this are particularly pertinent at the present moment, as these organic particles contain carbon. Globally, vast amounts of carbon are locked up in this organic matter. It has been estimated that soils around the world contain approximately 2,000 billion tonnes of carbon in various forms at any one time. About 300 billion tonnes can be found as detritus in the topsoil.

This carbon-rich material decomposes at various rates, depending on factors such as temperature and soil conditions. The overall carbon content of soils has, in recent years, become seriously depleted. The slash-and-burn destruction of forests, as well as industrialised methods of farming, have drastically reduced the overall organic content of soil. Ploughing breaks the soil's surface and increases the rate of respiration, causing carbon to be leached into the air. Micro-organisms at work in the topsoil also return considerable amounts of carbon to the atmosphere in the form of carbon dioxide.

Researchers are developing ways to increase the carbon content of soils. When converted into an inert form, it can remain locked away from the atmosphere for thousands of years. As well as reducing the amount of greenhouses gasses in the atmosphere, such sequestration can improve the soil and its ability to grow plants.

Beneath the carbon-rich topsoil at Lower Treculliacks is a more dense and stony subsoil. The border between these different layers is surprisingly distinct, given the length of time that this ground has remained undisturbed. There is a clear visual demarcation between the brown and yellow layers. The grey clays and yellowish brown lower soil show little or no infiltration from the dark brown layers above. It is highly compacted and very hard to dig. Small chunks of quartz sparkle in the sun and occasionally the spade hits a larger chunk of pinkish grey granite. As far as organic colonisation goes, these layers are as different as a fertile river delta and a parched desert. The density of this lower layer explains why water collects and drains only slowly from hollows in the field.

Underneath these layers of earth lies a massive slab of granite that, in places, protrudes through the grass. This igneous rock bubbled to the surface 300 million years ago, and formed a mountain chain. Over this unimaginable period of time these hard rocks have been slowly folded and contorted. In its early history this land was once an arid desert, in equatorial latitudes. Today, erosion and continental movement, has left the gently contoured landscape that is typical of the region.

With these and other various particles of knowledge we can know something of the history of the place, and how it came to be. With a geological eye we can track its formation and genesis. We can assess what plants will naturally grow well, and which are likely to fail. We can see which minerals are lacking and supplement them in order to manage and maintain a healthy balance.

Although this knowledge is helpful to the gardener and farmer, soil is more than simply the medium upon which terrestrial life depends. The various soils of our planet are not just clays and grits that contain organic matter and support plants. They are living entities that can only be fully appreciated in a holistic way. The fungi, bacteria, arthropods, nematodes, earthworms and even moles are all dependent on one another and the medium that supports them. Soil is so much more than the sum of its mineral and organic constituents; it is perhaps best understood as an inter-acting community of living events – a super-organism.

Although we now know more about the workings of the soil than ever before, our culture continues to misuse it and abuse it. We have come to treat it as an expendable commodity, as mere dirt. Yet history tells us that a culture that mistreats its soil will not be around for long.[8] We could do well to re-discover our deep-rooted connection with earth.

## Language of dirt

Despite the scientific and artistic interest in this material, soil is still not generally held in high esteem. One only has to reflect on the English language to understand the lowly place of mud in our culture. For example, most dictionaries, in addition to defining the noun 'soil' as the portion of the earth that consists of disintegrated rock and humus, also refer to soil as a verb, which generally means 'to make unclean', or 'cover in excrement'. To soil something is to stain it, and this is equally true of someone's character as it is of his or her clothing. To soil someone's good name is to morally defile them.

The word 'mud' has similar connotations. To say that someone's 'name is mud' is to say that it is tarnished and disgraced. Similarly, when someone has become 'muddled' they are mentally confused. The word 'dirt' has even more negative connotations. Being dirty is equivalent to being rude in most contemporary contexts, and to call someone 'dirt' would imply that they are worthless. One of the most significant implications of this use of language is the notion that soil and its associations are bad and should be avoided. So how did this happen and, more importantly, what are the consequences of such negative associations?

As huge populations began to drift towards cities and away from any direct contact with non-urban settings, there was less need to touch soil. Indeed, the aspiration of many was to do exactly that, to avoid getting their hands dirty. No doubt this was, in part, a move away from the poverty and harshness experienced by many previous generations of farmers and land labourers. The majority of adults no longer need to get their hands dirty on a daily basis. Even children are persuaded, by cultural, parental and peer-group pressure to play indoors or on artificial surfaces. Fewer and fewer sports take place in muddy fields.[9]

This lack of contact with the soil is a relatively modern phenomenon. For most of the history of humanity, certainly since farming became widespread, soil would have been seen as a vital material and, in some cases, a sacred one. Although it is hard to ascertain, it is likely that most pre-modern cultures revered the planet and its soil. This is perhaps most poetically expressed in biblical stories of the first human, Adam. Although scholars still debate the origins of the name, many believe that it is derived from the Hebrew word 'adamah', meaning 'earth' or 'soil'. Adam's co-occupant and mate, Eve, was originally called 'Hava', which translates as 'living'. The original people were, in this biblical account, named after the living soil.

Numerous other cultures similarly embed the sacredness of soil in their myths and legends. The indigenous peoples of Australia, Africa and America all sanctified and revered the earth. This view is eloquently expressed by Chief Seattle in his dignified reply to the United States government when it sought to acquire native lands: "We are part of the earth and it is part of us… What befalls the earth befalls all the sons of the earth…To harm earth is to heap contempt upon its creator".[10]

Even today, this connection between humanity and earth is not lost in the language used by gardeners. The 'humus' that constitutes a healthy soil shares a common root to our word 'human'. As we degrade and poison the life-giving humus, we are in danger of losing our humility and our humanity. As more and more topsoil gets blown away in dust storms, we should remember that we not only lose our ability to sustain ourselves, but we actually lose our very substance. Now, more than ever, the need to rehabilitate the language and substance of mud becomes increasingly urgent.

## Thinking soil

It is vital that we take care and look after our soils. We need healthy soil to sustain plant growth and to provide a global carbon sink. But we also need, now more than ever, to renew and maintain a deep or spiritual relationship with earth. Getting to know the soils beneath our feet can provide a method for reconnecting with our source and our sustainer.

Ultimately, we need to protect the soil because it is our home. We came from it and we shall return to it. However far we stray, in the end we always come back. And not only is it our home, the soil is also in us. As with all living organisms, we are not simply dependent upon this planet, we are quite literally made from it, our bodies are composed of it – we can never really be apart <u>from</u> it for we are very much a part <u>of</u> it. And, despite our technological prowess – which frequently serves to distance us from the soil – we still remain intimately connected to this earth from which we emerged.

If soil is conceived as a super-organism – as more than the sum of its parts – it remains essentially amorphous, without an overriding form. We, descendents from the living earth, are that aspect of the soil that has taken form – that has pulled itself together and learnt to move around. We are soil that has learnt to talk and reflect on its place in the cosmos. We are walking, talking, thinking soil.

6    John Evelyn. *Terra, a Philosophical Discourse of Earth*. 1675, quoted in Sir E. John Russell, *The World of the Soil*, p.1.

7    The Munsell system is a colour space that specifies colours based on three colour dimensions, hue, value (or lightness), and chroma (roughly saturation). It was created by Professor Albert H. Munsell in the first decade of the 20th century, and is now widely used for matching soil colours.

8    See: Daniel Hillel. *Out of the Earth: Civilisation and the life of the soil.* London: Aurum Press, 1992.

9    For a thorough examination of the disasterous consequences of allowing children to lose touch with nature see: Richard Louv. *Last Child in the Woods*. Algonquin Books, 2006.

10 Although there is some dispute as to the exact content of Chief Seattle's speech, which was given in 1854, the popularity of this text reflects the respect that an aboriginal people feel towards the land on which they dwell.

**Books consulted while researching this project:**

Yvonne Baskin. *Under Ground: How creatures of mud and dirt shape our world*. Washington: Island Press, 2005.

John Stewart Collis. *The Worm Forgives the Plough*. Harmondsworth: Penguin, 1973.

Daniel Hillel. *Out of the Earth: Civilisation and the life of the soil*. London: Aurum Press, 1992.

Sir E. John Russell. *The World of the Soil*. London: Collins, 1957.

Amy Stewart. *The Earth Moved*. London: Frances Lincoln, 2004.

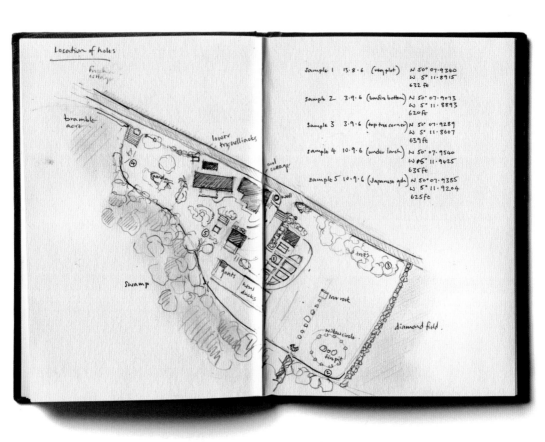

Location of holes

Frenchie cottage

bramble
acre

lower trevelliacks

oval cottage

well

swamp

goats

hens
ducks

trees

love rock

willow circle

fire pit

diamond field.

Sample 1  13·8·6 (veg plot)  N 50° 07·9340
                                  W 5° 11·8915
                                  632 ft

Sample 2  3·9·6 (bonfire bottom)  N 50° 07·9073
                                    W 5° 11·8893
                                  620 ft

Sample 3  3·9·6 (top tree corner)  N 50° 07·9289
                                    W 5° 11·8607
                                  639 ft

Sample 4  10·9·6 (under larch)  N 50° 07·9540
                                    W 05° 11·9425
                                  635 ft

Sample 5  10·9·6 (Japanese gdn)  N 50° 07·9385
                                    W 5° 11·9204
                                  625 ft

*'Nature is not a place to visit, it is home.'*
Gary Snyder

Five sites were chosen from different
locations to give a variety of soil samples.
These sites provided examples of land that          LOCATING
had been both cultivated and left
uncultivated. They included dry ground,
wet ground, woodland and pasture.
Between them they represent the variety
of soils present at Lower Treculliacks.

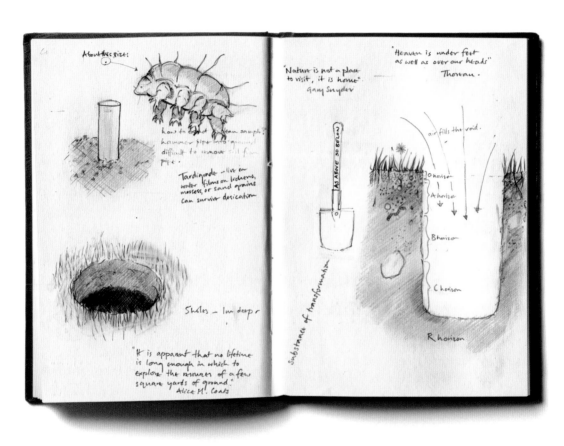

About this size:

how to collect clean sample?
hammer pipe into ground,
difficult to remove soil from
pipe.

Tardigrade — live in
water films on lichens,
mosses, or sand grains
Can survive desiccation

Shales — 1m deep r

"It is apparent that no lifetime
is long enough in which to
explore the minutes of a few
square yards of ground."
Alice M. Coats

"Nature is not a place
to visit, it is home".
Gary Snyder

"Heaven is under feet
as well as over our heads"
Thoreau.

AS ABOVE SO BELOW

substance of transformation

air fills the void.

O horizon
A horizon
B horizon
C horizon
R horizon

*'To forget how to dig the earth and to tend the soil is to forget ourselves.'*
Mahatma Ghandi

The initial core was extracted by driving a pipe into the ground. However, the integrity of the sample was damaged by its removal from the pipe. Subsequent cores were taken by digging a hole 1 metre deep and extracting the soil carefully with a shovel. This was then preserved in a wooden box.

COLLECTING

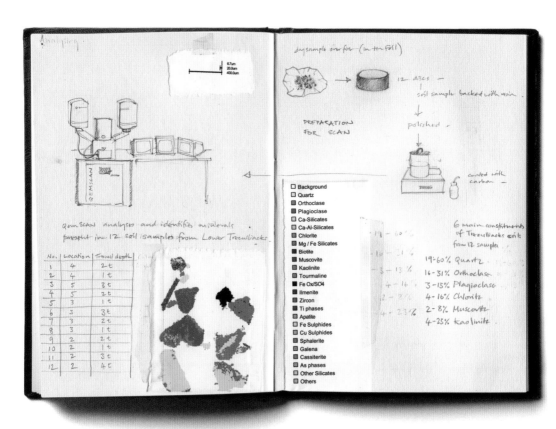

Sampling:

6.7um
20.0um
400.0um

QEMSCAN

QemSCAN analyses and identifies minerals
present in 12 soil samples from Lower Trecullacks.

| No. | Location | Trowel depth |
|---|---|---|
| 1 | 4 | 2t |
| 2 | 4 | 1t |
| 3 | 5 | 3t |
| 4 | 5 | 2t |
| 5 | 3 | 1t |
| 6 | 3 | 3t |
| 7 | 3 | 2t |
| 8 | 3 | 1t |
| 9 | 2 | 2t |
| 10 | 2 | 1t |
| 11 | 2 | 3t |
| 12 | 2 | 4t |

dry sample over fire (in tin foil)

→     12 discs —

soil sample backed with resin

PREPARATION
FOR SCAN

↓

polished —

coated with carbon —

☐ Background
☐ Quartz
☐ Orthoclase
☐ Plagioclase
☐ Ca-Silicates
☐ Ca-Al-Silicates
☐ Chlorite
☐ Mg / Fe Silicates
☐ Biotite
☐ Muscovite
☐ Kaolinite
☐ Tourmaline
☐ Fe Ox/SO4
☐ Ilmenite
☐ Zircon
☐ Ti phases
☐ Apatite
☐ Fe Sulphides
☐ Cu Sulphides
☐ Sphalerite
☐ Galena
☐ Cassiterite
☐ As phases
☐ Other Silicates
☐ Others

6 main constituents
of Trecullacks soil
from 12 sample

19-60% Quartz.
16-31% Orthoclase.
3-13% Plagioclase
4-16% Chlorite
2-8% Muscovite
4-25% Kaolinite.

*'This field is a laboratory; it is a store house of food; it is a reservoir; it is the nursery of battalions of bacteria in ceaseless chase; it is the habitation of countless worms who swallow it. It is a vast potential.'*

John Stewart Collis

Twelve small samples were taken from the cores and dried over a fire. These were then prepared in the laboratory for various types of analysis. The topsoil was found to contain considerable amounts of organic matter to a depth of 40cm. The most abundant minerals found in the soil were quartz, orthoclase, plagioclase, chlorite, muscovite and kaolinite.

ANALYSING

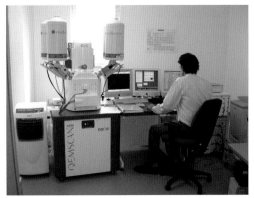

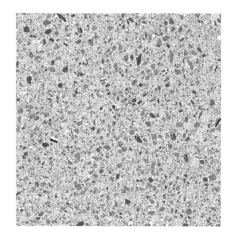

Background
Quartz
Orthoclase
Plagioclase
Ca-Silicates
Ca-Al-Silicates
Chlorite
Mg / Fe Silicates
Biotite
Muscovite
Kaolinite
Tourmaline
Fe Ox/SO4
Ilmenite
Zircon
Ti phases
Apatite
Fe Sulphides
Cu Sulphides
Sphalerite
Galena
Cassiterite
Other Silicates
Others

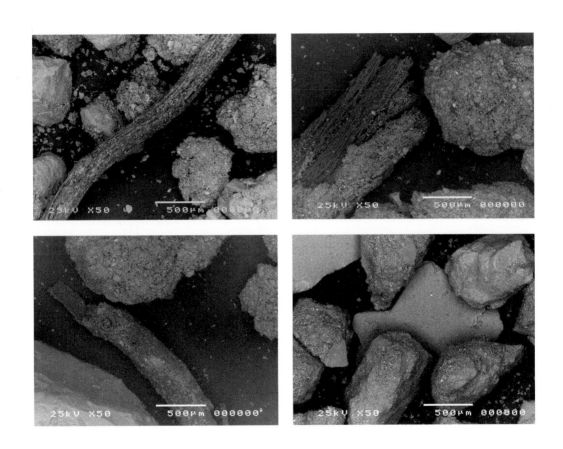

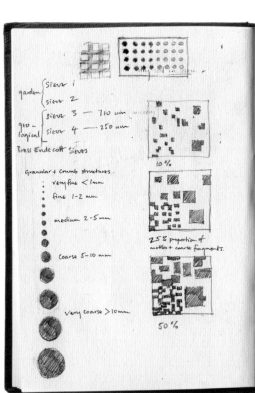

garden { sieve 1
         sieve 2

geo- { sieve 3 — 710 um (microns)
logical { sieve 4 — 250 um

Brass Endecott sieves

Granular + crumb structures.

· very fine < 1mm

• fine 1-2 mm

● medium 2-5 mm

● coarse 5-10 mm

● Very coarse > 10mm

10 %

25 % proportion of
mottles + coarse fragments.

50 %

8 colours of Treculliacks -

| 12 | Light Brownish Grey | 10YR | 6 / 2 |
| 3 | Pale Brown | 10YR | 6 / 3 |
| 1,9 | Light Yellowish Brown | 10YR | 6 / 4 |
| 6,7 | Yellowish Brown | 10YR | 5 / 4 |
| 2,5 | Dark Greyish Brown | 10YR | 4 / 2 |
| 10 | Brown | 10YR | 4 / 3 |
| 8,11 | Very Dark Greyish Brown | 10YR | 3 / 2 |
| 4 | Light Olive Brown | 2·5Y | 5 / 3 |

HUE    VALUE   CHROMA
(yellow
red)

Munsell Colour System

HUE - its relation to Red, Yellow, Green, Blue, Purple
VALUE - indicates its lightness
CHROMA - indicates its strength (or departure
from a neutral of the same lightness)

| CONDITION | Dark (dark grey; Brown to black) | Moderately dark (brown to yellow brown) | Light (pale brown to yellow) |
| --- | --- | --- | --- |
| organic matter | high | med | low |
| erosion factor | low | med | high |
| aeration | high | med | low |
| available nitrogen | high | med | low |
| fertility | high | med | low |

"The names for soil colours are common
terms now so defined as to obtain
uniformity and yet accord, as nearly
as possible with past usage by soil scientists.
Names like 'rusty brown', 'mouse grey', 'lemon
yellow, and chocolate brown should never be used"

*'Soil… scoop up a handful of the magic stuff. Look at it closely. What wonders it holds as it lies there in your palm.'*

Stuart Maddox Masters

The samples were sorted by particle size and colour. The dried mud was sieved into four separate sizes that ranged from 8mm to 250um (microns). Using the Munsell colour system, the palette at Lower Treculliacks was found to consist of eight distinct colours that range from light olive brown, through yellowish brown to dark greyish brown.

SORTING

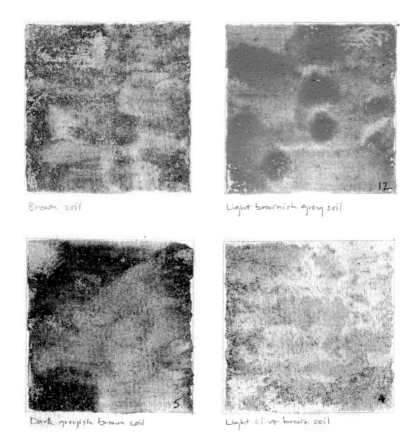

Brown soil

Light brownish grey soil

Dark greyish brown soil

Light olive brown soil

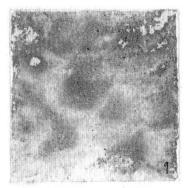

Light yellowish brown soil

Pale Brown soil

Very dark greyish brown soil

Yellowish brown soil

Creating.

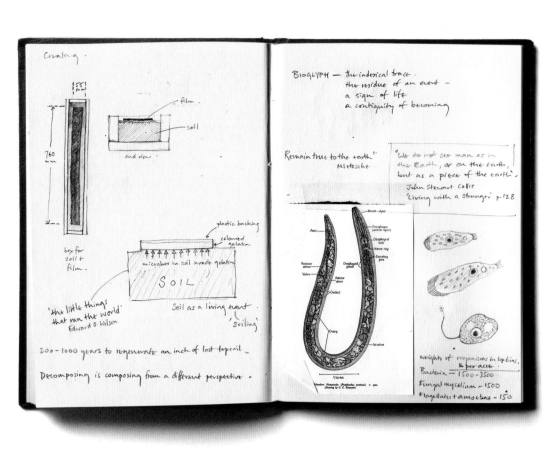

|← 55 →|
mm

760
mm

box for
soil +
film.

film.

soil

end view.

plastic backing
coloured
gelatin

microbes in soil invade gelatin
↑ ↑ ↑ ↑ ↑ ↑ ↑ ↑ ↑
SOIL

Soil as a living event.
'soiling'

'the little things
that run the world'
Edward O. Wilson

200 - 1000 years to regenerate an inch of lost topsoil.

Decomposing is composing from a different perspective.

BIOGLYPH — the indexical trace.
the residue of an event —
a sign of life
a contiguity of becoming

"Remain true to the earth."
Nietzsche

"We do not see man as in
the Earth, or on the Earth,
but as a piece of the Earth".
John Stewart Collis
'Living with a stranger' p.128

Mouth-stylet
Oesophagus
(anterior region)
Anus
Oesophageal
bulb
Nerve-ring
Excretory
pore
Posterior
uterus
Oesophageal
glands
Valve
Anterior
uterus
Oviduct
Ovary
Intestine

⊢——⊣
1/10 mm

Meadow Nematode (Pratylenchus pratensis) × 500.
(Drawing by C. C. Doncaster)

Weights of organisms in top 6 ins.
lb per acre
Bacteria — 1500 - 3500
Fungal mycelium — 1500
Flagellates + amoebae — 150

*'Given only the health of the soil, nothing that
dies is dead for very long.'*
Wendell Berry

Five prepared films were encased in
wooden boxes with the soil cores to create
Bioglyphs. After four weeks the films were
extracted, dried and viewed on a
microscope. Photographs of small sections
of the film were made with a diameter of
approximately 2mm.

CREATING

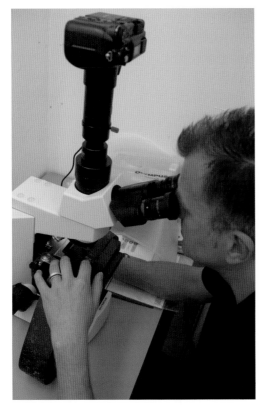

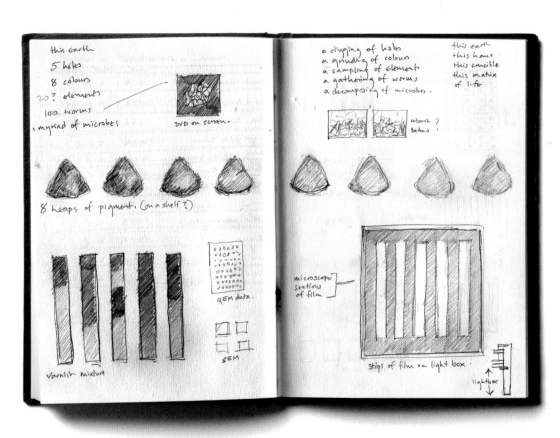

*'Most of all one discovers that the soil does not stay the same but, like anything alive, is always changing and telling its own story. Soil is the substance of transformation.'*
Carol Williams

The work was presented at Sherborne House in Dorset at the Future Palette exhibition. The gallery became the artist's studio for the duration of the exhibition. As well as finished artworks, the exhibition included the soil samples, maps, photographs, scientific data, tools, equipment and a gardening jacket.

PRESENTING

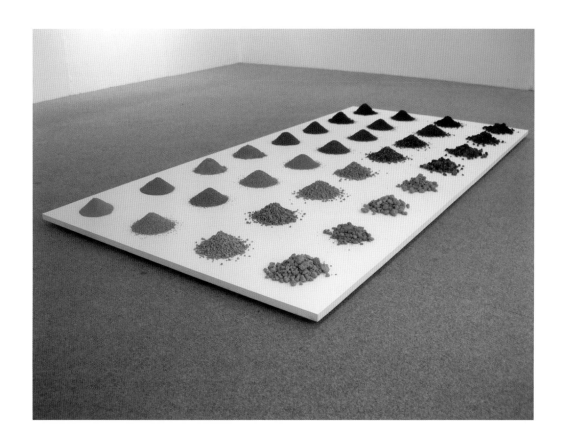

*'We do not see man as in the earth, or on the earth, but as a piece of the earth.'*

John Stewart Collis

THIS EARTH 2006

Five strips of buried film on a lightbox.
Ten framed digital prints.

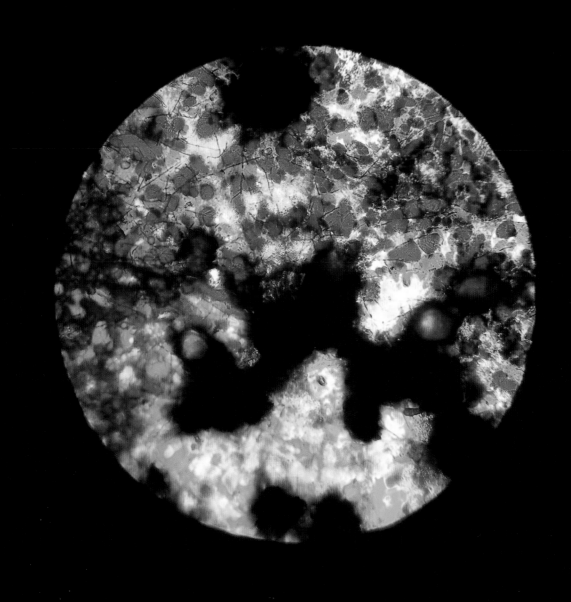

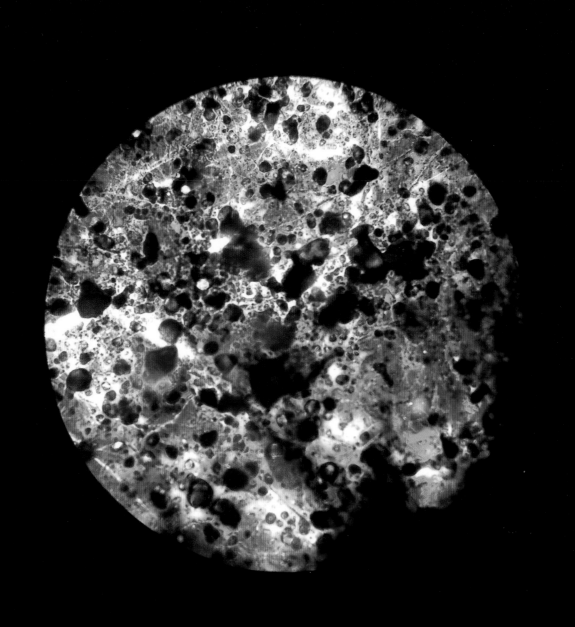

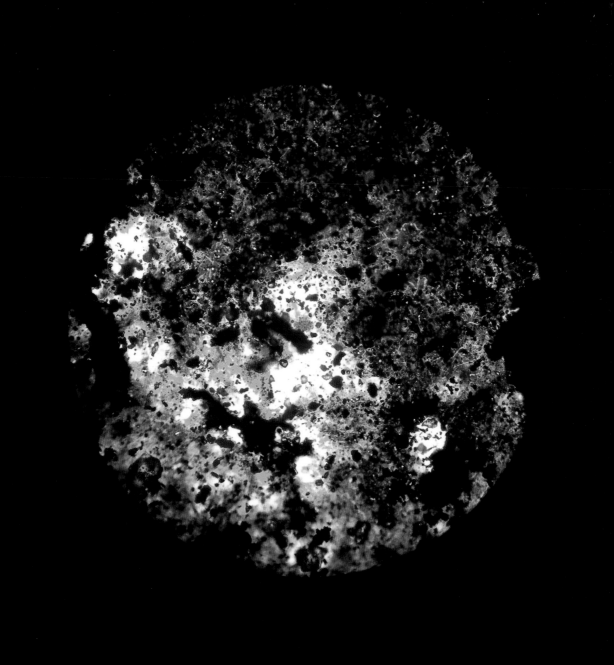

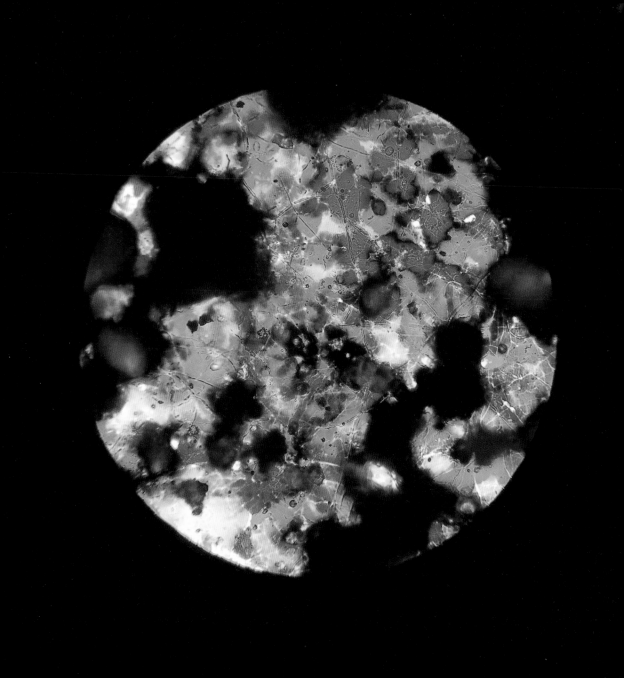

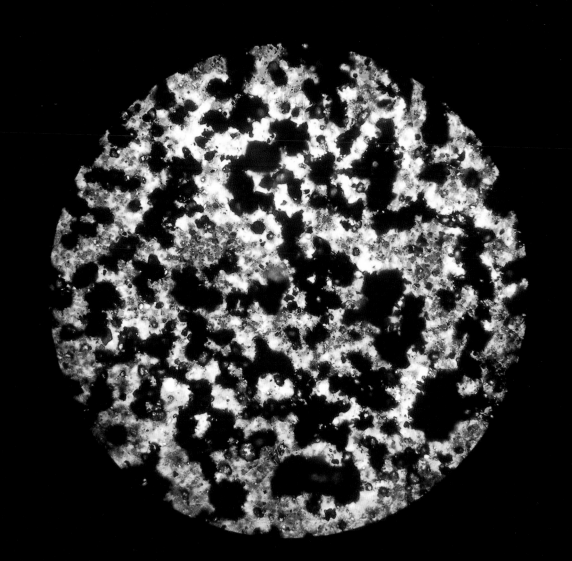

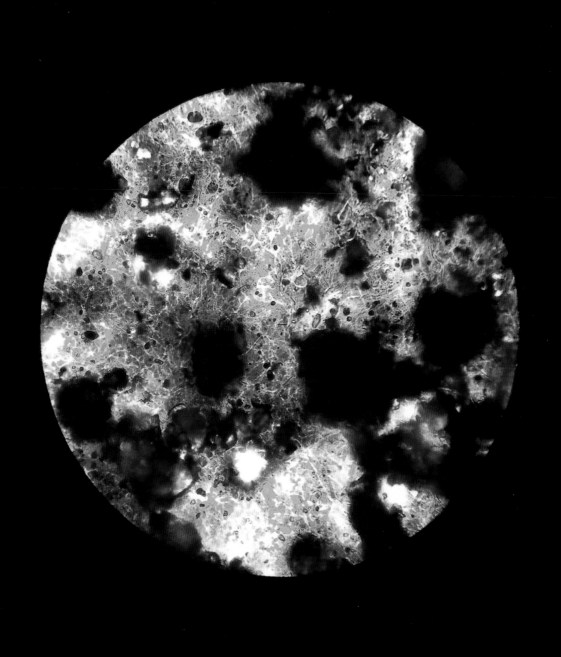

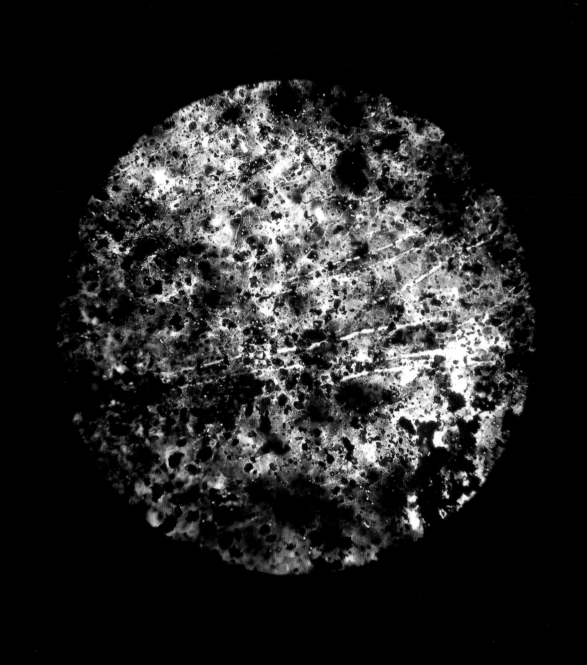

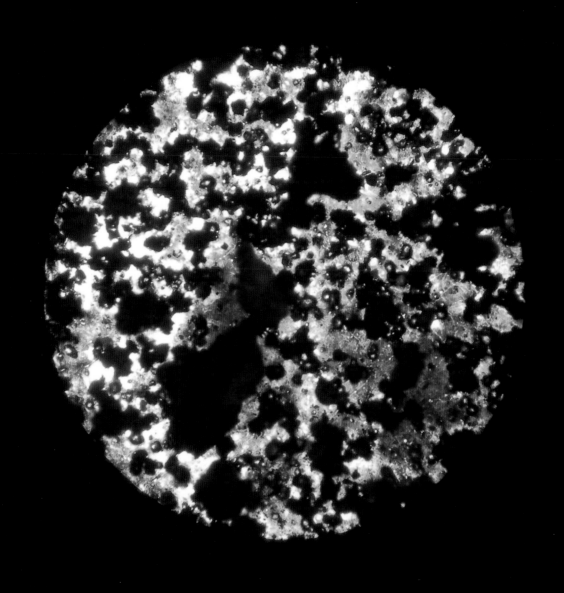

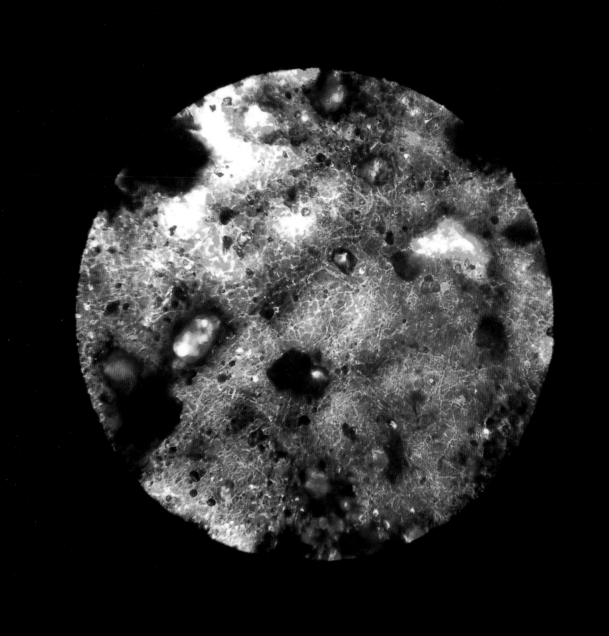

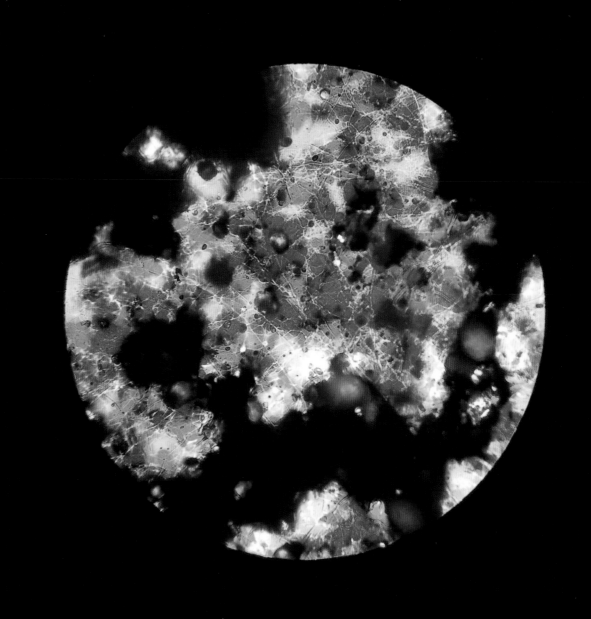

Daro Montag makes art with living matter. His research and creative practice start from the premise that the natural world is best understood as being constituted of interacting events, rather than consisting of discrete objects. This philosophical position foregrounds the importance of process and its residue in our understanding of nature. Over the past twenty years the artist has enlisted the assistance of micro-organisms, plants, insects, toads and other living matter. His current practice examines the ecology of his home environment.

Daro completed his MA at the Royal College of Art in 1994 and a PhD at the University of Hertfordshire in 2000. His work has been exhibited at galleries in the UK, USA, Europe and the UAE, and published in a number of catalogues. In 2002 he was awarded a prestigious art-science prize in Tokyo. In the same year he was commissioned to create a new work, in collaboration with the Institute for Animal Health, for an exhibition on the aftermath of the outbreak of Foot and Mouth Disease. In 2004 he created work that records the activities of the wind and rain, for an exhibition at the Met Office and, in 2006, was commissioned by Sherborne House to produce a project on the theme of 'Colour & Chemistry'. The Sherborne House commission led to this publication.

Daro lives and works in Cornwall where he leads the MA Fine Art, and the RANE research cluster, at University College Falmouth.

*This Earth* was first exhibited as part of Future Palette exhibition,
Sherborne House, Dorset, in October–November 2006.

The work was also shown as part of Deep Process exhibition,
Gershman Y Gallery, Philadelphia, USA in February 2007.

Prints can be viewed at Purdy Hicks Gallery, London. *www.purdyhicks.com*

*The artist would like to thank:*
Dr Matthew Power and Dr Gavyn Rollinson – scientific analysis, Camborne School of Mines
Ken Gadd – scientific support, 4science
Bryony Bond – exhibition curator, Sherborne House
Ros Marchant and Amanda Wallwork – project co-ordination, Sherborne House
Stig Evans and Balint Bolygo – artists involved in Future Palette
Robin Hawes – research assistant

This project has been supported by RANE (Research in Art, Nature & Environment) at University College Falmouth.

University College
**FALMOUTH**

R A N E
**Research in Art,
Nature & Environment**

**Sherborne House**

EUROPEAN UNION
European Social Fund

www.falmouth.ac.uk

www.rane-research.org